A Listen to

WORLD
music

Written by
Jennifer Reed

Rourke
Educational Media

rourkeeducationalmedia.com

www.rourkeeducationalmedia.com

PHOTO CREDITS: Cover: © Alan Crawford (top left), © Cristian Lazzari (bottom left), © desifoto (top right, bottom right), © DNY59 (center globe); page 1: © amfroey; page 4: © guenterguni; page 5: © Grigorios Moraitis; page 6: © THEGIFT777; page 7: © narvikk (top right), © Steve Evans (bottom left), © Antonella865 (bottom right); page 8, 9: © Derejeb; page 10: © cristianl; page 11: © hadynyah; page 12: © lisafx; page 13: © 1001nights; page 14: © Angela Ostafichuk; page 15: © Christophe Boisvieux; page16: © Patricia Hofmeester (top left), © rosta (bottom left), © Tepic (bottom right); page 17: © Mastering_Microstock, Featureflash (inset); page 18: © Herwig Prammer; page 19: © GA161076 (top left), © Jinlide (top right), © Ravindran John Smith (bottom); page 20, 21: © fritz16; page 22: © Guangliang Huo

Edited by Precious McKenzie

Cover and Interior design by Tara Raymo

Library of Congress PCN Data

A Listen to World Music / Jennifer Reed
(Art and Music)
ISBN 978-1-62169-879-1 (hard cover)
ISBN 978-1-62169-774-9 (soft cover)
ISBN 978-1-62169-979-8 (e-Book)
Library of Congress Control Number: 2013936788

Also Available as:

Rourke Educational Media
Printed in the United States of America,
North Mankato, Minnesota

rourkeeducationalmedia.com

customerservice@rourkeeducationalmedia.com • PO Box 643328 Vero Beach, Florida 32964

TABLE OF CONTENTS

MUSIC OF THE WORLD

People all over the world love to **sing** and **dance**. World **music** is truly the music of the entire world!

World music may be sung or played on instruments. Each culture creates music in its own way.

Ethnomusicology is the study of world music. Let's learn about world music.

Many colleges offer world music in their music programs. These classes study both music and cultures from around the world.

SOUNDS OF AFRICA

There are many regions in Africa. Each region has its own **culture**. Each culture has its own type of music.

NORTH AMERICA

SOUTH AMERICA

EUROPE

ASIA

AFRICA

Ethiopia

AUSTRALIA

Ethiopia is a country in Africa. Some **instruments** found in Ethiopia are the krar, the begenna, the masenko, and drums. A reed-like flute might be played by shepherd boys tending to their cattle.

Drum

Krar

Horn

Both traditional and modern Ethiopian music is played for entertainment at **festivals** and weddings. Ethiopians love their traditional music, which itself has only five notes: do, re, mi, fa, so, and la.

TILAHUN GESSESSE
1940-2009

Tilahun Gessesse became a famous Ethiopian musician in the 1960s. This time period was considered the golden age of Ethiopian music. He soon earned the nickname "The Voice" because he loved to sing. He often raised money by singing so he could help his people during hard times.

Latin Music

Four regions make up Latin America. They include Mexico, Central America, the Caribbean Islands, and South America. Each country and region has its own culture and own style of music. Instruments may vary greatly from region to region. The most common instruments include drums, guitars, xylophones, and flutes.

Peru is a country in South America. Long ago, the Incas played the pan flute. Today, ancient music is still played. The Incas had only five notes, which often gave the music an eerie sound. They also had only four types of songs: songs about religion, war, mourning, or farming.

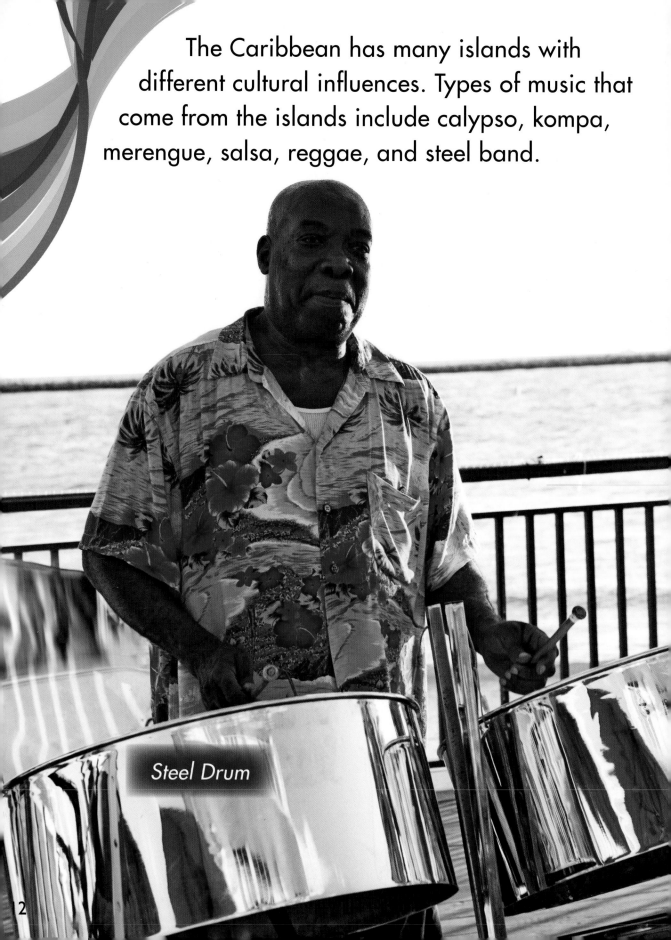

The Caribbean has many islands with different cultural influences. Types of music that come from the islands include calypso, kompa, merengue, salsa, reggae, and steel band.

Steel Drum

The music often echoes the carefree lifestyles of the warm Caribbean. Music from this area often features drums and singing. Many people like to dance to the music as it is usually fast-paced and upbeat.

Music from well-known Latin-American musicians like Celia Cruz and Tito Puente make up the daily lives of people living and traveling all over the world today.

CELTIC SOUNDS

Did you know that Celtic music comes from other places besides Ireland? Other areas that play and sing Celtic music include Scotland, the Isle of Mann, Cornwall, and Wales. Cape Breton, in Canada, is known as the Celtic capital of North America.

NORTH AMERICA

Cape Breton

Scotland
Isle of Mann
Ireland
Cornwall
Wales
EUROPE

ASIA

AFRICA

SOUTH AMERICA

AUSTRALIA

Celtic music stems from orally-transmitted traditional music. The types of music played include jigs, reels, ballads, hornpipes, polkas, and slow airs. Celtic songs are about the hardships and happier times of the people.

Bagpipes

Many instruments are used to create Celtic music. You have probably seen the bagpipes of Scotland, but many regions use another form of bagpipes. Harps, fiddles, drums, and flutes are also commonly used.

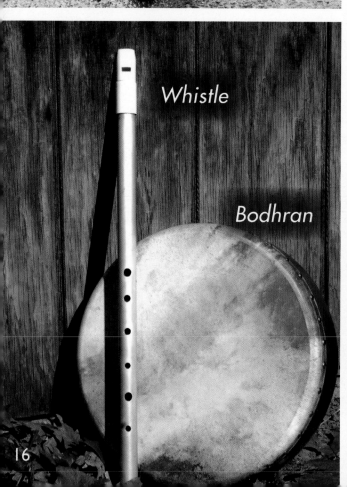
Whistle

Bodhran

Harp

Celtic music is popular today because people like to sing and dance to the music. Irish step dancing is believed to have come from traditional Irish music. The dances are also called jigs, slip jigs, reels, and hornpipes just like the music.

Celtic music has become popular in recent years because of musical groups like Celtic Woman, Enya, and Celtic Thunder.

Enya (1961-)

MUSIC OF ASIA AND THE PACIFIC

Countries in Asia and the Pacific have their own unique style of music and instruments. Indian classical music is most often played on a sitar. It is a plucked instrument, like a guitar, only much more difficult to play.

Ravi Shankar (1920-2012) was a famous sitar player from India.

Shamisen

Taiko drum

Min'yo is Japan's folk music. It is often played with a shamisen, drums, and a flute called a shakuhachi.

The most popular form of Indonesian music is called gamelan. Drums, xylophones, bamboo flutes, and gongs make up gamelan.

Kendang

Metallophone

AUSTRALIAN SONGS

One of the most familiar forms of music from Australia is music of the **Aborigines**. In Australia, bush music has been handed down from generation to generation. The songs were often based on life in the bush, or on the land.

The most famous
Australian folk song
is Waltzing Matilda.
It is known as a
bush ballad. It is
often played on the
didgeridoo, which is
a wind instrument.

Didgeridoo

21

There is beautiful music being made all over the world. It is yours to explore!

The guzheng, a traditional Chinese instrument, has 18 strings and movable bridges.

GLOSSARY

Aborigines (ab-UH-rij-uh-nees): native Australians

culture (KUHL-chur): characteristics of a particular group, often includes language, food, religion, and music

dance (dahns): movements that match the rhythm of music

ethnomusicology (eth-NOH-myoo-zi-kol-uh-jee): the study of world music

festivals (fes-tuh-vuhlz): events where music is played

instruments (in-STRUH-muhnts): tools used to create music

music (myoo-ZIK): the art of sound using voice and instruments

sing (SING): to use voice to produce sounds in musical tones

INDEX

WEBSITES

mamalisa.com

www.centerforworldmusic.org

worldmusiccentral.org

ABOUT THE AUTHOR

Jennifer Reed lived in Japan for 3 years and often listened to Min'yo. She has traveled to many countries and listens to world music. She even tried to play a didgeridoo in Australia. These days, Jennifer prefers to play the piano or sing in a choir. She also writes many books for children.

Meet The Author!
www.meetREMauthors.com